CONSIDER

*Questions
That Make You
Think*

BARBARA ANN KIPFER

Random House Reference

New York • Toronto • London • Sydney • Auckland

RANDOM HOUSE is a registered trademark of Random House, Inc.

Please address inquiries about electronic licensing of any products for use on a network, in software or on CD-ROM to the Subsidiary Rights Department, Random House Information Group, fax 212-572-6003.

This book is available at special discounts for bulk purchases for sales promotions or premiums. Special editions, including personalized covers, excerpts of existing books, and corporate imprints, can be created in large quantities for special needs. For more information, write to Random House, Inc., Special Markets/ Premium Sales, 1745 Broadway, MD 6-2, New York, NY 10019 or e-mail specialmarkets@randomhouse.com.

Visit the Random House Reference Web site: www.randomwords.com

Library of Congress Cataloging-in-Publication Data

Kipfer, Barbara Ann.
  Consider this— : questions that make you think / by Barbara Ann Kipfer.
    p. cm.
  ISBN 978-0-375-72198-4 (trade pbk. : alk. paper) 1. Philosophy--Miscellanea.
I. Title.
  BD31.K56 2007
  100--dc22

                        2007003098

Printed in the United States of America

10 9 8 7 6 5 4 3 2

Dedication

To my husband, Paul Magoulas.

No one thinks quite like you!

INTRODUCTION

Philosophy is intriguing to all of us. Every day, without realizing it, we play the role of "philosopher" by asking ourselves and others questions: *Why do I have such bad luck? Will I ever meet my soulmate?* or by listening to others pose questions on television or radio and in newspapers or books: *Are we brainwashed by advertising? Are scientific facts always reliable?* We like to think about the questions, the puzzles, the conundrums, the enigmas.

CONSIDER THIS . . . is a collection of the little questions, the big questions, philosophical thoughts, timeless puzzles, and those nagging questions that comedians often ask and we laugh at, but honestly don't know the answer to! Compiled in one book are over a thousand entries that will prompt and prod your mind. Discuss them with your friends and family, or simply ponder them yourself. As long as it gets you thinking. . . .

TABLE OF CONTENTS

The Arts

Is art an integral part of life?

Is beauty ageless?

Is art a craft or a science?

Can a human being produce
   something that is perfect?

Does inspiration "come" to a
   person or is it found through
   searching?

What is talent?

Is reading a good book like being
  with a friend?

What is it about beauty that draws
  us to it?

Is being beautiful an advantage or
  disadvantage?

What makes a book a classic?

Will creativity ever hit a ceiling?

Is there another word for
synonym?

Is it a fact or mere myth that the
artist suffers?

Is what we look like in the mirror
the same as what we look like to
other people?

Is what you look like an important
aspect of life?

*When does sound
    become music?*

What is the most superior art
form?

What role does fine art play in
our lives?

Can art really be judged?

Do things exist that we are unable
to perceive with our senses?

What motivates an artist?

In a song, which is more
   important, the music or
   the words?

Is the goal of art to be beautiful?

What is simple?

What areas of research should be
   broadened?

What does it mean that a work of
   fine art "says" something?

Should art be for art's sake?

Does listening to music help study
and memory?

Can language be exact and
express philosophical truth?

Is man the only species that can
enjoy beauty?

Does creativity recycle itself?

How do you know that you see
    the color blue the way that
    someone else does?

How does language connect us to
    the world?

How do words get their meaning?

What is the meaning of art?

Are works of art in the mind?

What makes something beautiful?

What is the distinction between
good art and bad art?

Can quality be defined?

Does true beauty need makeup?

How do children learn language?

Are artistic judgments subjective?

Is art serious?

What does art teach?

Describe "the simple life" in
  three words.

What is the importance of art?

Is beauty in the eye of the
  beholder?

How does art affect life?

Is the real voyage of discovery
   seeing with new eyes?

Is cooking an art?

Can you carry beauty with you
   instead of searching for it
   elsewhere?

What is it about creativity that
   brings us so much satisfaction?

Has everything already been written?

Can art be defined by a standard formula?

Can progress be made in art?

Is bad art still art?

Can talent be taught?

Is insanity a key to genius?

Is there more to the world than
just what we hear and see?

What is perfection?

Does imagination have limits?

Is it possible to have a keen vision
of all that is ordinary in life—
like hearing the grass grow?

Is thinking done in words?

Does language get in the way
of self-knowledge?

What is pure perception?

Can progress be made in
literature?

Does originality exist?

Do the arts have a destabilizing
effect on society?

Do blind people dream of objects
and colors?

Which came first—language or the
ability to categorize?

What is imagination?

How do we perceive the sound of
one hand clapping?

Will there ever be nothing left to
discover?

Is language pictorial?

What would be the advantages and
disadvantages of one language
for the whole world?

Cause and Effect

Do societies shape people or do
people shape societies?

Why should one person obey
another?

Does time erode all achievements?

Does will drive behavior?

Are there problems that can't
be solved?

If a tree falls in the woods and
   nobody is there to hear it, does
   it make any sound?

Where does karma come from?

Do we possess free will?

Do you believe in self-fulfilling
   prophesy?

When is surrender a weakness and
   when is it a strength?

Does an antagonist help in
strengthening your nerves and
sharpening your skill?

Is change predictable and
reversible?

How long does it take to become
enlightened?

Does anyone have the right to tell
another person what to do?

Are all of our actions determined
by heredity and environment?

How can there be free will if
everything is scientifically
determined?

What great thing would you
attempt if you knew you could
not fail?

Does every event have a cause?

Can voyages be accomplished
inwardly?

How do you measure a person's success in life?

What is a brave act?

What exactly is the mind-body relationship?

Are we always influenced by the actions and reactions of others?

Is it possible to achieve everything?

Do excuses erase
responsibility?

What is a miracle?

Are miracles logically impossible?

What is the purpose of dreaming?

Is man merely a product of his
education?

What kind of "life food" are you
eating and digesting?

How do people learn?

How can you make a difference
in this world?

What determines human
behavior?

What was the first "cause"?

Can there be many paths to a
single goal?

How would you distinguish
between logical and natural
necessity?

What responsibilities never cease?

How can we know what one's
intention is at any particular
time?

Do people have full control over
their actions?

Do you ever think about how you
  positively or negatively impact
  the lives of those around you?

Is it possible to be lonely in a
  crowd of friends or family?

Is it easy to live simply?

Are there causal determinants of
  choice?

Do thoughts create dreams or
  dreams create thoughts?

What factors and conditions are indispensable to progress?

Is there a logical conflict between the notions of change and sameness?

Are we aware of the real causes of our actions?

What is the primary aim of education?

What is the difference between work and play?

How much responsibility do we
    have for things that happen
    to us?

Can a mental event be affected by
    a physical event?

Do past actions account for
    present and future situations?

Do we control what we think or
    does what we think control us?

Is moderate behavior the goal of
    mental health?

*Does everything
in life have
a purpose?*

Do you believe that meditation is
   an effective form of recharging?

Can an event be non-causal?

Can thinking about something
   make it happen?

What is the pattern of change that
   takes place in time?

Does karma exist?

What is destiny?

Do you believe in destiny?

Can anyone predict the future?

Do you believe in "every man
for himself"?

Can taking the initiative get you
into trouble?

Should people be held
    accountable for the
    consequences of what happens
    if nothing is done?

What is fate?

Do you believe in fate?

Is pride in what you are doing one
    of the greatest sources of
    energy?

Do you believe in nature or
    nurture?

Is it the grain of sand in your shoe
  that wears you out?

Does one work for the sake of
  having free time or does one
  have free time from working?

Is everything in flux?

Are all things intricately
  connected?

Is the lust for power rooted in
  weakness or strength?

Which is more important, leisure or work?

If you try to fail, and succeed,
which have you done?

Should wealthy people be
required to financially help
out poor people?

Does winning ever teach us
a lesson?

Is life a fixed creation or an
ever-evolving process?

Is there a pattern to change?

Can waiting too long to take action
get you into trouble?

What caused the universe to exist?

Can we ever escape change?

Is our behavior directed by will?

Do you believe in the power of
self-transformation?

Can there be liberty apart from equality and fraternity?

Is progress necessary and inevitable or is it the result of people exercising their freedom?

When is work not work?

Is a teacher supposed to learn more than she teaches or teach more than she learns?

Does the end always justify the means?

Does a person create his or her own destiny?

How can a just and fair world be created so there are not any causes for terrorism?

Do we resent or envy people who are able to slack off?

How do you know if you are
   putting enough into life?

Why do you use harsh words?

Is education the key to freedom?

If quitters never win, and winners
   never quit, then why should you
   quit while you're ahead?

Have you ever noticed that
   anybody going slower than you
   is an idiot, and anyone going
   faster than you is a maniac?

Why is it that when you're driving
and looking for an address, you
turn down the volume on the
radio?

Does one need grounds for doubt?

How do we know when something
is worth trying?

Do we pay for our mistakes?

*What is the greatest
    gift a person can
give to another?*

Existence and Death

What is existence?

What is a soul?

How do you answer the question:
    Who am I?

Does everything that happens
    repeat itself eternally?

When is life not worth living?

Can a person who died, still, in
    some way, be alive?

Is there a way of proving some
    "thing" does not exist?

Does the self continue beyond
    death?

Where does our soul come from?

What is death?

If reincarnation exists, why is there
   no remembrance of past lives?

How old is old?

Is everyone equal at birth?

What are the moral arguments for
   an afterlife?

Do things exist as you perceive
   them?

How long does something stay
    new?

Is there anything we must do while
    we are alive?

Why does anything exist at all?

Do we have to experience
    something in order to know it
    exists?

Should one tell a dying person the
    truth of his or her condition?

Can anything be and not be at the
same time?

Does death give life meaning?

Is it right to sacrifice the life of
one conjoined twin in order to
save the other?

Can the soul exist before birth and
after death of the body?

Has "being" ceased to have any
meaning?

Can something that is not a
    material object have real
    existence?

Can someone have knowledge
    of their own death?

Are all humans related?

Does anything exist of necessity?

Do we take anything with us
    when we die?

Does life have a cycle of birth, death, and rebirth?

Did man come to exist by God's creation or through the processes of natural selection?

Are humans the only species that questions why they exist?

Should assisted suicide be permissible?

*What would
happen if people
lived forever?*

What is the goal of life?

Why does the world exist?

Is it really important to know why
    we exist?

Does the awareness of death create
    fear and anxiety?

Is there any logic in the existence
    of life?

Do we have a say in the world
   we are entering?

Does life have value?

Why is there anything at all?

Is death the great equalizer?

What is the nature of whatever
   it is that exists?

What does it mean to die?

Do you consider suicide to
be murder?

Do ghosts exist?

What gives life meaning?

Is the soul immortal?

Why are most deaths sad?

Does the soul remain constant
throughout life?

Is death a precursor to new life?

Can the human soul be
reincarnated and reborn as
an animal?

Is life a continuous, progressive chain?

Why does society try to prolong life for terminally ill people?

What is the difference between existence and essence?

Can you doubt your own existence?

What is the best way to die?

Is a wrongfully prolonged life as
    tragic an error as a wrongfully
    terminated life?

Is everything that exists a "what"?

Can euthanasia be justified?

Why is death feared so much?

Is there a heaven?

Can we achieve nirvana?

What is the difference between
being and becoming?

Could we always be dreaming?

Is capital punishment murder?

Do we have the ability to
communicate with the dead?

Is all philosophy a response to the question of death?

Can intelligent life ever pass away completely?

Who is a funeral for: The person who died or the people left behind?

Is it possible for people to die before their time?

Does fear prevent us from living
life to the fullest?

What are the limits of human
endurance?

What is the moral meaning of an
unnatural death?

Does disease recognize borders,
race, or religion?

What exactly is "nothing"?

Is death like birth?

Can you die of over-
encouragement?

Do we live in dreams?

What will happen to the world
when you die?

Good and Evil

Is justice enough to make society
serve its human purpose?

Is human nature inherently good
or bad?

Are defects always bad?

Are people bound by moral laws?

How does personal development
occur?

Are all of us lovable?

By what standard are laws good
   or bad, just or unjust,
   expedient or inexpedient?

Can goodness be taught?

Can there be a utopia?

What is a just person?

What is bad?

Is it possible to have justice for all?

What creates hatred?

Is it possible to live with no
    regrets?

Do we need to ask anyone whether
    something is right or wrong or
    deep down do we know?

Is prudence itself a virtue?

Can a defeat be more triumphant
than a victory?

How many heroes remain
unknown?

Is most of the world's evil done
by evil people?

Can there be good without evil?

Why would God allow evil to exist?

Does omnibenevolence entail
    benevolence toward bad things?

What do we seek to achieve
    by punishing?

Is the impulse to destroy a
    universal enemy?

Where does morality come from?

Is there such a thing as competing
basic moral standards?

Is morality simply a matter of
prejudice or can we give good
reasons for our moral beliefs?

Is caring for others a selfless act?

Are we here for a greater purpose?

*Why do bad
things happen
to good people?*

Are wars necessary in order to
achieve peace?

What is good?

Are all living beings Buddhas,
endowed with wisdom
and virtue?

What is hell?

Can an animal be evil?

Is torture ever justified?

Do people have heroes or
heroines anymore?

How does prudence, an
intellectual and moral
virtue, differ from art, an
intellectual virtue?

Is violence entertaining?
If so, why?

Is the distinction between
　morality and politeness
　merely an illusion?

Is the majority always right?

What is the difference between
　loving goodwill and just
　goodwill?

Can a universally just and
　civil society ever be achieved
　by mankind?

What are the causes of conflict?

Which is better, to do injustice to others or to suffer injustice?

Can morality be taught?

What is moral justification?

Is morality based on religious concepts?

Is failure always bad and success always good?

Can some human beings obey or disobey laws as they choose?

Why should we be moral?

What are values?

What values are most important?

What constitutes the "good life"?

Should we help other people who have made "wrong" decisions in life?

Which virtues should we adopt?

Is it possible to derive a moral value purely from a statement of fact?

Does justice treat everyone fairly?

Is there any virtue that isn't initially, if only in some small way, a desire for virtue?

How do you know "right" from "wrong"?

What is the difference between an intellectual virtue and a moral virtue?

If a friend betrays you, is it wise to continue trusting the friend?

Are good deeds rewarded? Are bad deeds punishable?

Which is more populated: heaven or hell?

Is the difference between good
    and evil a matter of opinion?

Is all knowledge good?

How can equality be achieved?

How can you be a good person?

Are we born with a set of basic
    morals and ethics or are they
    learned?

Do we have an innate sense of
    what is right and what is wrong?

Do we call something good
    because we desire it or do we
    desire something because it
    is good?

Is there some good in all human
    beings?

How can morality function in a
    world governed by scientific
    laws?

What is justice?

Can good be done in a wrong way?

Can someone be completely good
    or completely evil?

Is justice an unobtainable ideal?

What does it mean to live with
    integrity?

*Is love a weakness
or strength?*

Is there an unchanging standard
   of morality that applies to all
   people throughout the world?

Do people generally have
   common courtesy and
   manners?

How do you explain why any bad
   people live long, happy lives
   while good people die at an
   early age?

What does it mean to act selfishly?

Do we ultimately always act out of self-interest?

How do you know what is right?

How should we treat other people?

How do evil and suffering fit into the divine plan?

Do people tend to inflict more pain or create more pleasure in others?

Are there different types and
degrees of alienation?

Is it easier to do good or evil?

Can a concept like self-deceit be
possible?

Is justice itself subordinate to the
general good?

Can we pursue a common good?

What kinds of good come from
difficult situations?

Is life a test?

Is it possible to live authentically?

Why do we get pangs of guilt?

What is the highest virtue?

Can men and women ever achieve true equality?

How can tyranny exist in this day and age?

What is morality?

What counts as harm?

How does our understanding of what is right and wrong lead to an understanding of justice?

How do we know that our
behavior is ethical?

What is the highest human
aspiration?

Is humble pie comfort food?

Is the courage to do evil,
still courage?

Is there such a thing as "good
crazy"?

*How much
of life is just
plain luck,
good or bad?*

What does being courageous
   require?

How do we decide which is
   correct when the arguments are
   equally good on both sides?

Is God powerful enough to
   eliminate evil?

Has society issued laws that
   conflict with morality?

Why do we punish? What do we seek to achieve?

How can we know when we are right?

Are most people who are considered "great people" morally admirable human beings?

How can you help others if you cannot help yourself?

Is justice enough to make a good society?

What does the merciful person think about?

What acts do you consider to be unforgivable?

Is the universe a battleground between the forces of good and evil?

Do we have a duty to volunteer?

Would you stand up for something
you thought was right, even
though many may disagree?

Is there natural justice?

How do we become just,
temperate, and brave?

*When is honesty
not the best policy?*

When is a terrorist not a
    freedom fighter?

Is everything of value valued
    for a reason?

Is it difficult to tell the difference
    between a charlatan and
    a prophet?

Is it always reasonable to be
    reasonable?

Is it ever right to break a promise?

What is grace?

Are we capable of doing evil
without realizing it?

If everyone thinks you are
wrong, are you wrong?

Happiness
and Suffering

Is ignorance bliss?

Does desire cause suffering?

Must we suffer?

How are the different kinds of love
related to one another?

Can we really love our neighbor
as we love ourselves?

Is getting what we want worth
the trouble?

Are the three greatest lessons
simplicity, patience, and
compassion?

Do our passions lead us astray?

Can you ever have it all?

Can you ever have too much?

Do you agree or disagree that it is important to have a good hard failure when you are young?

Do desires prevent us from achieving tranquility?

Is money an aphrodisiac?

Is there a moral consequence for economic growth?

Does everything have a price?

Why does happiness seem to last
    such a short time?

Do all people suffer equally?

What is success?

How can we tame the rat race?

Do people want more or
    enjoy more?

How does someone know if they
have become enlightened?

Can someone force themselves
to be free?

When is enough enough?

What does it mean to be content?

Does being tolerant mean
tolerating everything?

Is sexual pleasure like the
    pleasure one gets from eating
    and drinking?

Why do you want to be happy?

What does it mean to be gifted?

When does a passion become
    a vice?

Are men and women alike in
    their desires?

Are play and leisure different
    things?

What is friendship?

What is real happiness?

Can any desire be ever fully
    satisfied?

Does economic growth make
    society more materialistic?

Why do so many people seek counseling?

Is love ever born of desire or
    desire of love?

Are you in control of your
    own life?

Why do some people suffer
    so much?

Is writing your own epitaph a
    great way of finding out what
    you want from life?

Do you believe that playing is
    more important than winning?

What is the greatest pleasure
in life?

Do individuals struggle to create
meaning for themselves?

Do capitalism and materialism
prevent us from satisfying our
natural minds?

Do we choose to love?

Does the brain look for the
    most rewarding view of
    circumstances?

Is it better to have loved and lost
    than never to have loved at all?

Is emotion the opposite of reason?

What are natural human desires?

Do only the unlucky or unworthy
    suffer defeat?

Which produces more pleasure;
    to love or to be loved?

Is the glass half empty or half full?

How is a person to lead a
    happy life in a dangerous and
    unstable world?

Do all humans have a desire
    for power?

Are the best things in life free?

Do we tend to only pay attention
to what matters to us?

Can love be studied scientifically?

Is your job meant to be fulfilling?

Is the limitlessness of desire a
disease of the imagination?

Is happiness the same for all or
does each person seek it
according to his own desires
and judgments?

What is the path to liberation?

Can a collective happiness ever
    exist in the world?

Can a selfish person achieve true
    self-realization?

Why is it better to relieve our
    hunger and thirst than to rid
    ourselves of melancholy?

Can a dream be taken away?

What makes something funny?

Is it better to live a short and
    happy life or a long and
    unhappy one?

Do you agree that the good things
    in life are either immoral,
    illegal, fattening, or unhealthy?

Which is the stronger emotion:
    anger or love?

Can hatred be studied
    scientifically?

Can enlightenment be achieved
    without realizing it?

Is pity a selfless sentiment?

Do people tend to find something
    desirable in almost any
    negative circumstance?

Is happiness always the goal?

If you do not get it from yourself,
    where will you go for it?

Is it better to have goals?

Is contentment a positive or
    negative characteristic?

Should you just enjoy your ice
    cream while you are eating
    it or think about why you're
    enjoying it?

What is more important: love
    or success?

Is there a fair way to quarrel?

Is happiness objective or
   subjective?

Does philosophizing make
   people happier?

What ultimately prompts our
   desires?

Is there anything that is good
   for everyone?

How do you know when you are
   in love?

What is love?

Why does love exist?

Does joy just come upon you or is it a controlled decision?

Why do we purchase so many material things that we will never use?

Does private property help or hinder human development?

Will everything you demand and even get eventually disappoint you?

Can love be measured?

Can human beings make each
other happy?

What is the nature of the union
that lovers seek?

Why does love hurt?

Does a meaningful life require
meaningful work?

Can suffering be measured?

Does poverty diminish human
dignity?

Why do we have a right to
pursue happiness?

In this world, is it "every man
for himself"?

What causes people to be hopeful?

What is the greatest gift a person
can give another person?

Are life's gifts obvious?

For what might one claim
exclusive rights to another
person?

Is true love possible without being
loved in return?

How is it that some of us feel pain
less but make more fuss?

Can friendships be momentary?

Is happiness genetic?

Is sex ever simple?

Does dessert satisfy a biological
or social need?

Is it okay to avoid work if we
can get away with it?

Do thought-provoking jobs help
    prevent senility and dementia
    as we age?

What is the most crucial step
    toward solving a problem?

What is the ultimate antidote
    to fear?

What is the most invincible
    kind of strength?

Can you allow yourself to
    be happy?

The world seems to have become
    addicted to self-improvement—
    but is it any better for it?

What is the best thing that a
    marriage can be based on?

Are parents ever to be faulted for
    the failure of their children?

Ideas and Opinions

Can insanity bring on more
 creativity?

Can someone be sane and
 insane at the same time?

How are our thoughts derived?

Can the outcome of any choice
 be certain?

Is it better to be ignorant or
    in error?

Where does human knowledge
    come from?

How has experience determined
    our attitudes and beliefs?

What makes a big question
    in life big?

Do we have the right to believe
in things without sufficient
evidence?

Does anybody ever realize how
little they know and how much
they have to learn?

What are ideas?

Can something other than a
human be considered a friend?

Can you articulate your most
  fundamental beliefs and the
  reasons you hold them?

How rational are humans?

What is the scope of knowledge?

Are there thoughts that cannot be
  expressed in any language?

How does someone obtain peace
  of mind?

How are friendships different from other types of relationships?

Is it easy to be certain?

Is knowledge rooted in sense perception?

Is it a talent to use one word instead of two?

How do we tell whether our opinions are objective or subjective?

Does everyone have a philosophy
of life?

Is meaning always the product
of interpretation?

Can emptiness be experienced?

What is the basis of the knowledge
of self?

What makes two people friends?

Is it possible to think about nothing?

Is the mind, in any sense,
    mechanical?

How much of our time is spent
    thinking about ourselves? Is it
    too much or too little?

If a thought cannot be clearly
    stated, what value is it?

At what point do people have the
    right to attempt to overthrow
    their government?

Is learning hard work?

How can one swear to love
     another forever and to love
     no one else?

What is good faith?

Is it possible to instinctively
     know what another person
     is thinking?

Is there any type of knowledge
     we should not seek?

Why do some people feel a need
to justify their beliefs?

Are things interpreted the same
way each time?

Is being skeptical about knowledge
a sign of intelligence or a sign
of ignorance?

What are friends for?

Is war a political policy?

Is academic intelligence better than life experience?

Do we have a finite or infinite number of beliefs?

What is the difference between thinking and reasoning?

Are more people lazy or hardworking? Why is this?

What is the essence of belief?

How do we know
that memory is ever
really reliable?

Is decision-making the most
important human activity?

Is the modern mind the same
as the ancient mind?

Can you have your cake and
eat it, too?

Is genius created or born?

Is knowledge power?

What is the examined life?

Why question?

Can you legitimately answer a
  question with a question?

Can fear influence your ability to
  know and understand things?

Are all things inhabited by a soul
  or spirit?

Is it easy to forgive yourself?

Can a human ever achieve
perfect understanding?

Can quality be measured?

How do people become wise?

What percentage of life
is wasted?

What is so common about
common sense?

How do we know anything?

Can walking spur creative ideas?

What was the most important idea
of this century?

What was the most important idea
of the last century?

What was the most important
theory of all time?

How do we acquire reliable
knowledge of the world?

Can your "mind's eye" see as
much as your real ones?

How can thinking skills be
acquired?

Is it possible to be too curious?

Are human beings nature's most
important creation?

Can enlightenment be achieved
by anyone?

What is man's ultimate goal
with technology?

Can a dream lie?

Should there be legal limits
to the amount of pay a CEO
of a company makes?

*What is meant
by genius?*

Who is in charge: man or
    machine?

Can anyone be sane in this world?

Do the mind and body ever
    disagree?

Can adults think like children?

Are computers more intelligent
    than humans?

Does the mind contain more
    than we are aware of?

Why is yawning contagious?

Who are five people that
    define style?

Can technology surpass human
    intelligence?

Can any one thing be seen
    by two minds in the same
    way simultaneously?

Is there dignity in all kinds of
    work?

Is technology a double-edged
    sword?

Why do some countries drive on
    the left while most other
    countries drive on the right?

Are members of a royal family
    born with special rights?

Are we all brainwashed by
   advertising?

Did you ever feel that the world is
   a tuxedo and you are a pair of
   brown shoes?

Are we here to embrace or
   conquer the world?

Why do you so often see one shoe
   lying on the side of the road?

Why do we cry?

Do children profit from the
experience of their parents?

Does modern technology put
more people out of work or
create more jobs?

Who has the unfair advantage:
men or women?

Can an opinion be true or false?

What is the difference between
    an emotion and a feeling?

Is there such a thing as an
    original thought?

Is affirmative action a form of
    discrimination?

Can something outrageous
    eventually appear reasonable?

*Is the whole
more than
the sum of
its parts?*

Do people have a right to
control other people?

What do women really want
from men?

Are things usually more or less
complicated than they appear?

Can you feel pain when you
are unconscious?

Can the whole be defined by
its parts?

Can something logical not
    make sense?

Is the mind an active or passive
    receptor and processor of data?

Can the mind be observed?

How is youth viewed in old age?

How much does the body
    influence the mind?

Should people risk their lives for something that they believe in?

Is there a ceiling on how much you can know?

Is stubbornness always a negative quality?

When is a person's sexual orientation determined?

Is the existence of a government imperative to achieving an ordered society?

Is our brain more like a computer or is a computer more like our brain?

How do beliefs about what is valuable influence the pursuit of knowledge?

What do men really want from women?

What is normal?

Can emotions be measured?

What is a home?

Do exams truly test one's
intelligence?

Is it better to be wanted or
needed?

Does a wise person change his or
her mind frequently?

Is parenting a competitive sport?

Can there ever be an anti-
addiction pill?

Does watching a lot of television
make a person less intelligent?

If you learn something, are
you wiser?

Is it possible to live with no regrets?

How much of life is choice and
how much is luck?

How can the imagination be
improved?

What was the best thing before
sliced bread?

Why don't you ever see the
headline "Psychic Wins
Lottery"?

What makes a person exceptional?

Is there such a thing as a one-sided friendship?

What makes a person interesting?

Why do we laugh when someone falls?

Nature and Animals

Can anything change human
   nature?

Can the universe be explained in
   mathematical terms?

Do we have soul mates?

How is human progress measured?

Are some dimensions of
   personality common across a
   wide range of species?

How is a person's identity
   established?

What is nature's greatest sound?

Can an animal find something
   funny?

What is a civilized society?

Do other living organisms
   besides human beings have
   the freedom to act?

What is the difference between a
human being and a robot?

Is man good by nature?

Can animals love?

Do humans possess a collective
unconscious?

Do civilizations advance by leaps
and bounds or gradually?

*Are humans capable
of mastering nature?*

How do new traits emerge
in species?

Is intelligent life designed for
us to study it?

By nature, do we all want to
be happy?

Is there a future for gene therapy?

Does disease periodically cleanse
the world?

Why do children wonder
   ceaselessly?

Does nature follow universal laws?

Can man be entrusted with the
   preservation of the world?

Do societies try to control the
   behavior of their population?

How come no two humans are
   identical?

What would it take for us all to just get along?

Is the mind a blank slate when we are born?

Is it morally acceptable to genetically design children?

Was man different in degree or kind from the anthropoid apes?

Why do we age?

Is the earth a living, self-regulating organism?

Is social chaos worse than tyranny?

Which came first, the chicken or the egg?

Would clones have the same dreams?

Is the human condition constrained by outside forces?

*Is there certainty
in science?*

Do humans have a self-destructive
   nature?

Do you think God designates how
   long each person will live or
   does he allow circumstances to
   determine longevity?

Is it necessary for personality
   to exist?

Is it ethical to breed animals
   for human consumption and
   clothing materials?

Are humans nothing more than
elaborate machines?

Are the material resources of
the world finite?

Why do gender relations exist
in society?

Are children born with an innate
knowledge about how language
works?

Are certain nationalities, races, religions, political parties, or countries better, smarter, more industrious, and more efficient than others?

How much of human behavior depends on genes?

What is a family?

Why is decision-making an important human activity?

Are animals entitled to certain
basic rights by virtue of being
sentient, social creatures
capable of emotion and pain?

Do adults produce children or
do children produce adults?

Is a human's life more important
than an animal's life?

Is it the same when a human
kills to eat meat as when an
animal does?

Is every human being shaped exclusively by his or her environment?

Is human emotion always rational?

Can a conflict-free society exist?

If a person's mind is transferred
  to a new body, would it still be
  the same person?

Do trees and plants have souls?

Do humans have infinite abilities?

Why is man the sacred animal of
   the west, while in the east,
   monkeys and cattle are more
   sacred than humans?

Are human beings part of nature's
   great recycling system?

Is man embedded in nature?

Is everything in nature useful?

Can an animal be a judge of
   beauty?

Do most societies display
ethnocentric attitudes?

Can you ever really "be yourself"
when you are with others?

Should we modify the climate?

Why don't we feel bodily
processes like blood moving
from one chamber of the
heart to another?

Can one person be more
   important than another
   person?

Has there been progress in human
   nature over the years?

Are genetic differences between
   races biologically important
   or unimportant?

Are we imprisoned in our
   own bodies?

*Can people achieve
perfect health?*

Are genes destiny?

Is natural selection a great idea?

Could animals believe in a
 higher being?

Can the same techniques for
 training animals be used to
 train people?

Can a scientific discovery ever end
the debate on evolution?

Should financial incentives
be used to increase organ
donation?

What do you do when you see an
endangered animal eating an
endangered plant?

Is sexual orientation based on
choice or biology?

Philosophy and Religion

Does the universe have intrinsic
  meaning?

Is science the new religion?

Are freedom and equality in
  conflict with one another?

Do humans have a love affair
  with the irrational?

Can the question of God ever
  be answered?

What is the relationship between
the spirit and matter?

Is there a lack of critical thinking
and judgment in the United
States today?

Can children be philosophers?

Is there a universal religious
impulse in humans?

Do philosophical ideas have a
  direct practical influence on
  human beings?

Is the unexamined life not
  worth living?

Since there are so many religions
  in the world, how does anyone
  know which one is the right
  one?

Why do we have laws and rules?

Are all religions essentially
the same?

Is the evidence of the natural
world sufficient to prove the
existence of God?

Is it better to ask questions or
know the answers?

Do you know how many "great
ideas" were initially laughed at?

Is civil law always an obstacle
    to freedom?

Can you explain logical positivism
    or moral relativism?

Why do people disagree so much
    on ethics?

What are the similarities between
    religion and philosophy?

Can progress be made in religion?

*What would
be empirical proof
of God's existence?*

What is society's greatest barrier
to peace?

Do we know and understand
what God wants?

Is religion a human invention
or a discovery?

Are ancient religious rituals still
important in modern times?

Can more than one religion
be correct?

Where did God come from?

Does each new answer prompt
  another question?

Is it ever legitimate for some
  people to have authority
  over others?

What is the relationship between
  God and nature?

What makes a question a
  philosophical question?

Why is it often the young who
   challenge the rules and
   regulations of society?

Why do philosophers talk so much
   about bizarre possibilities that
   other people happily ignore?

Does God reward and punish?

Is it reasonable to adhere to
   a religion?

Does science drain the world
   of moral purpose and spiritual
   meaning?

What does the phrase "We are all
   Buddhas" mean?

Has the course of history been
   shaped by or determined
   exceptional individuals?

Could science prove the accuracy
   of any religion?

How much power should
government have?

What constitutes a life well lived?

Can the existence of God ever
be proved?

Can majority rule be defended
as being on the side of wisdom
as well as being on the side
of freedom?

What is needed to make
   democracy work?

Should there be a legal drinking
   age?

Are wars outdated?

Is government necessary?

Is mathematics a human
   invention or a discovery?

Where is heaven?

Can there be more than one God?

Will belief in God ever die?

Is existentialism compatible
with ethics?

How big of a role do religions
have on shaping the
governments of the world?

What is a world view?

Is political controversy good?

Does something spur great
philosophical developments
or periods?

Does God have foreknowledge
of all events in eternity?

Is God observable?

*As a ruler, is it
better to be
loved or feared?*

Do all religions depart from the true way?

What would happen if an irresistible force met an immovable object?

Do we have a need for authority?

What is work?

Is belief the same as faith?

What makes a person spiritual?

What gives us the impulse to
    believe in God?

If there is a creator, who created
    the creator?

What are the best proofs that
    God does not exist?

Is the theory of intelligent design
    a challenge to the theory of
    evolution?

Is Buddhism a philosophy or a
    religion?

Is there no such thing as a foolish
    question?

How does the philosophy of
    history differ from history
    itself?

Do technological advances cause
   social changes?

How can you have a "civil" war?

Is war inevitable?

What starts most wars?

Why can't God make a perfect
   world?

Throughout history, has religion produced more good or more harm in the world?

Does "nowhere" exist?

If we can send a man to the
moon, why can't we make a
decent electric car?

What is the difference between
reason and faith?

Is Christianity a philosophical
religion?

Is life a mystery to be lived
or solved?

Does common sense offer us the
    greatest potential for
    understanding philosophy?

What is a world?

Has God abandoned man?

Why does Marx think human
    alienation can only be
    overcome in a classless society?

Does philosophy get closer and
closer to the ultimate truth as
time goes by?

What is genuine peace?

Is religious belief a predictable
by-product of ordinary
cognitive function?

With technology making
tremendous leaps and bounds,
will philosophy radically
change?

Do questions reveal more about
the world around us than the
answers?

What are the problems
with philosophy?

What is sacred?

Can philosophy be taught?

What is the most important
philosophical question?

What is the common goal of the
political community?

How can a scientific theory be
justified and accepted?

How do laws induce obedience?

What type of person is best
qualified to govern society?

Does science rule out or exclude
the existence of God?

Does youth teach us about
the future?

Is God's will known?

What are the differences between
internal and external freedom?

What contribution does
philosophy make to the world?

Are human rights universal?

What is philosophy's relevance?

Which holds greater hope for the
world: religion or science?

Will science ever help us achieve
immortality?

How can government serve
the common good when both
political parties take sides
on issues?

Are social practices justifiable?

Does Eastern philosophy influence
Western philosophy?

Does Western philosophy
influence Eastern philosophy?

Is commerce a means of social
control?

Is "I don't know" ever an
acceptable answer?

Is it easier to prove that God exists
or that God does not exist?

*Why does Sartre
say that we are
"condemned to be free"?*

Should political leaders always be
above military leaders or
should military leaders always
be above political leaders?

What are the pros and cons
of religion?

Can science and religion
happily coexist?

Are believers happier than
nonbelievers?

Why do some religions spread
   while others vanish?

How do you ask a difficult
   religious question?

Why do religions have elaborate
   social strictures, rituals, rules,
   and theologies?

Do you agree with the statement,
   "A leader who does not hesitate
   before he sends his nation into
   battle is not fit to be a leader"?

Time and Space

Is there anything outside
    the universe?

If the big bang theory is true,
    then what was the catalyst for
    the bang?

What is our importance in the
    grand scheme of the universe?

Where does past "time" go?

How big is infinite?

What is the greatest unsolved
mystery of all?

Is time destructive?

Is evolution necessary for
intelligence?

Does the universe exhibit
design and purpose?

Would it be wise to look into
the future?

Does the universe have
complementary polar forces
that resolve its tension and
conflict?

Is time real?

Will time travel ever be possible?

Is anything permanent?

*Does time speed
up with age?*

Is the world shrinking?

How will the universe end?

Can time be wasted?

Is time-reversal possible?

Are there other worlds that are
not accessible to us?

Do people move through time like
   they move through space?

How does the evolution of a
   species occur?

Can any moment ever repeat
   itself?

You can know light, but can you
   imagine what creates light?

Does each generation have
  its own unique philosophy?

Must we betray the past in order
  to love the present?

What is the maximum population
  the Earth can hold?

Can time be bought?

What was true of the universe at
time zero?

How do we know about abstract
concepts, like numbers?

Do celestial bodies influence
events on Earth?

Is the future infinitely long?

Does the Earth have its own
energy field that can be
released?

What is the perfect age and why?

Does time correct all scientific
  errors?

Was chaos the generating
  principle of the beginning?

Is there some type of intelligence
  behind the universe?

Can the future be predicted by
  looking back at history?

Is there more order or chaos
    in the universe?

Do aliens exist?

How does youth view old age?

Without knowledge of the past,
    would we have any knowledge
    at all?

How do you measure a lifetime?

*Are we alone
in the universe?*

If not now, when?

If the universe is everything,
and scientists say that the
universe is expanding, what
is it expanding into?

Can we ever experience equal
distribution throughout the
world?

What is time?

When should you stop being
youthful?

Truth and Reality

Can we answer any question
with certainty?

Is reality subjective?

What's in a name?

How can we be certain of
what we know?

What is truth?

Can you describe nothing?

Is awareness limited to
    experience?

What is absolute?

Do any two people experience the
    same event in the same way?

Is there more than one kind
    of truth?

What is the difference between
    reality and dreams?

Is life an adventure?

Is there more to reality than what
we can see and measure?

Can science explain the
supernatural?

Can there be *a priori* truths?

Can one have an out-of-body
experience?

Can we know something that has
   not yet been proven to be true?

Does truth matter?

Is reality only understood by
   explaining it in historical
   terms?

Are there universal moral truths?

How is truth recognized?

What is the relationship between
    facts and beliefs?

Do angels exist?

To what extent does our internal
    reality affect our perception of
    external reality?

Can an uncomfortable truth be
    evaded without doing wrong?

How does one study the
    supernatural?

Can we ignore basic facts and still
get to the truth?

What is a truthful person?

Is reality a continuum?

How do you distinguish reality
from appearance?

Are you fated to do certain things
with your life?

Is there more than one path
    to the truth?

Is logic somehow rooted in the
    structure of reality?

Does all reality become aesthetic?

Are scientific facts always reliable?

How can the truth be
    distinguished from falsehood?

How can we know that the
world as we take it to be, is the
world as it is?

Is reality meaningless?

Is being open to the truth easy?

Does each person in the world
have their own reality?

Does reality ever go away?

Is all truth relative?

How can one take something that
they find to be a profound and
universal truth and help others
to realize and understand it?

Do we have to think scientifically
in order to find the truth?

Can scientific facts change?

Can the truth ever be
renegotiated?

Can you discover your true
inner self?

Is anybody out there?

Are there real standards?

Why are things the way they are?

Can reality be found in the
    spiritual world?

What are the objectives in
    this world?

Are there any truths that all
humankind agrees on?

When is there enough evidence to
believe something is true?

Can ideas be the basis of reality?

Will there always be mystery
in life?

Is a city more than the people in
it, or are the people the city?

Can you prove that other life
    forms exist?

Do new times require new truths?

Are feelings real or imagined?

Is the only real fact that we exist?

Can you remember doing
    something that you, in fact,
    did not actually do?

Why do we like to escape
from reality?

Can a person prove they
are correct?

Can we know anything for sure?

If something cannot be disproved,
is it then true?

How do you know to trust
  someone?

How does science give us an
  objective view of reality?

Do solutions always breed new
  problems?

Do you agree with the statement,
  "If you can understand just one
  thing thoroughly, then you will
  understand everything"?

What is next?

ABOUT THE AUTHOR

Dr. Barbara Ann Kipfer is the author of more than 35 books, including the bestselling *14,000 Things to be Happy About.* Her other books include *Instant Karma, 8,789 Words of Wisdom, Self-Meditation, The Order of Things,* and *How It Happens.* Barbara has an MPhil and PhD in Linguistics from University of Exeter, a PhD in Archaeology and MA Buddhist Studies from Greenwich University, and a BS in Physical Education from Valparaiso University. Dr. Kipfer is the Managing Editor and Chief Lexicographer of Dictionary.com, Thesaurus.com, and Reference.com.